SEE THE PEOPLE

"How to target quality prospects and get in to see them."

BRUCE ETHERINGTON, BA, CLU, CHFC, CFP

For more information on the concepts presented in this book or additional copies, please contact:

Etherington & Vukets
12 Madison Avenue
Toronto, Ontario M5R 2S1
Canada

Telephone: (416) 351-1464
Fax: (416) 351-9535
E-mail: bruce@etheringtonvukets.com

Cover Design: Ken Harris Graphic Design

First printing, Singapore March 1996
Second printing, USA May 1996
Third printing, Canada May 1997
Fourth printing, Singapore February 2001
Fifth printing, USA August 2006
Sixth printing, USA June 2008

Printed in the USA

ISBN 0-9781821-0-3

To my wife, Karen
whose love
made this possible.

Because if we want to build relationships with our best clients, doesn't it make sense that we have to invest the time in order to get to know them?!

The Bottom 10

The bottom 10% of your clients (the "C" clients) are those to whom we know we have some type of responsibility, but who are not active with us and for whom we haven't found time to be proactive.

Yet, we continue to include them on our client list and, thus, allocate some service time towards, in the form of summaries and staff time, etc.

While we in the insurance business have an obligation to service our clients' policies, we also have a responsibility to run our businesses profitably. In order to effectively prune your garden over time, take this "10%" or, in fact, take a portion of your "C" clients and send them the following letter:

Dear John,

We note that we haven't had a meeting in the last three years. Please take a moment and cast your eye over the attached list. If you feel that one or two ideas may be of help to you and your family, please call as we'd be delighted to have a review with you

1. *$ at death to my family.*
2. *$ at disability and or critical illness to me and my family.*
3. *$ for my children's education*
4. *$ for retirement*
5. *$ sheltered from tax*
6. *$ for inheritance tax (capital gains and probate)*
7. *$ for charity*

On the other hand, if you don't wish to meet with us, please take a moment, sign this letter and return it to us and we shall close your file.

Best regards,

Bruce

You know what happens? You get a few people calling back for an appointment, and a few who send their letters back asking you to close their file.

But with the other 80% you've at least made contact and that's the secret. Your responsibility to "stay in touch" has been fulfilled and now "problem, problem who's got the problem?" ....

Over time, focus the structure of your business more and more on your "A" clients, while pruning your "C's" and "B's". In order to do this effectively you are going to want to associate with someone who has the time to service the "C's" and "B's" who want to meet with you and to whom you have promised to stay in touch.

However, the faster you can focus on the "acorns" who will become the "oak trees" rather than the "soft maples" that will have a limited life expectancy and profitability for your business, the better off you will be. As a matter of fact, the better off your clients will be also, and therein another principle of the "Golden Rule of Selling". Your clients will be better off because you will have the time to get to know and service them properly in a "high touch", "hands-on" manner.

For years I went around saying to myself: "I'm looking after Mr. and Mrs. Growing, but Mr. and Mrs. Stagnant, or Mr. and Mrs. Small Potatoes I'm not taking the time to see. I promised them I would but I haven't. I should be in touch with them, but when......?" (catch the guilt ball!!?)

If you can relate to this, then hopefully this will become a good way to stay in touch, while, at the same time, allowing you to begin pruning your "business garden."

Go back to your office, review your client files, rank them "A", "B", "C", and start the pruning process with your bottom 10%.

Your Top 20%

Take the top 20% of your clients, then rank them 1 through 40, 1 through 50, 1 through 100, however many that 20% may number. Then take the numerical Top 20 of the top 20%, call them and say

"John, I'd like to buy you breakfast or lunch".

At your meeting, while you are breaking bread, you ask your "Top 20 client" about his or her favourite subject - themselves - and get caught up on what's really happening in your clients' life.

For instance: Ask them the 3 year question (see chapter 13).

"So John, what's new, it's been a while since we last talked.

I just want you to know that you are a special client, you are important to me. What I would like to do over the years ahead is to get to know you better. Because as we both know there's a lot

ly? .... your business? .... your hobbies? .... your health? .... your friends? ..... .etc. etc."

And then at the end of the meeting as you pick up the check, you say:

"John, as you know, I'm in a people business. As a result I rely solely upon my clients for references to first class quality people like you, with whom to talk.

While I don't expect that you'll know anyone who's directly in the market for my products and services I do expect that you will associate with people, who like yourself, possess three basic fundamental characteristics.

#1. They are <u>responsible</u> family and business people, like you.

#2. They have the ability to <u>make a decision</u> based upon fact, as you do.

#3. They have outstanding economic <u>growth</u> potential, just like you.

So John, who are your three best friends, because I'd like to meet them?"

Recently, I did this with Mike, my client of 17 years and the conversation went like this:

"Bruce, how many years have you been looking after my insurance program?"

"Mike, you've been a client of mine for about 17 years."

"And how many people have I referred to you?"

"Mike, you've given me 15 terrific references over the years."

"OK, OK, I've got another one for you. But for goodness sake don't tell this person that he is my sixteenth best friend!"

Focus on your Top 20!

Prospect your Top 20.

Replicate your top 20 or better yet your top 5! As a result, you'll have 40 to 60 wonderful first class prospects within the first month to six weeks from the people with whom you love to do business - your "Top 20" !!

80-20-10!

80%	***Fewest results!***
20%	***Most results!***
10%	***No results!***

Focus on your top 20

Now calculate your average revenue per case and multiply it by your closing ratio times 40 to 60 prospects. That's what this idea is at least worth to you today.

Revenue Example

- $1,000 per case
- close 1/3
- Sales 1/3 x 60=20 x $1,000

=$20,000 Revenue

Plus Future prospects 3 x 20 = 60 etc.

6. Marlin

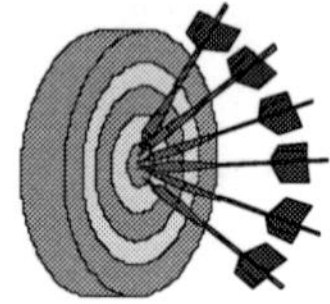

A number of years ago I asked Ron Barbaro, an early days mentor as well as the first Canadian to become President of the Million Dollar Round Table:

"How do I grow my business?"

Ron said. "How many of your clients are earning more than you are?"

To which I quickly and positively replied:

"None of them!"

His reaction stunned me:

"Kid, that is your first mistake. Think about it. If you're earning more than everybody you're talking with, then no matter how talented you may be, you're prospecting either "horizontally or down."

The secret to success in selling, particularly in the life insurance business, is to prospect up. So, figure out how to meet people who are either earning more money, or have more money than you."

What Ron was telling me, was that I needed to separate myself from the crowd by prospecting up instead of staying in my comfort zone and prospecting within it.

So, let's talk about fishing for **Marlin!**

You are already probably very good at doing some type of fishing in your business today, just as I was several years ago when I asked Ron that question. You see I was a really good "brook trout", "pan fish" (small fish) fisherman, who was able to catch a lot and eat regularly! However, I was focusing all of my time on the catching and none on the fishing, as mentioned previously, when we talked about "spear guns" vs. "fly fishing".

So in the "spirit of the tiger", don't make a 180 degree change in your business practice today. Instead, make a one degree change that over time will become two, three, four, five degrees or more by taking the time to get out of your comfort zone and go **Marlin** fishing.

Remember:
There are many more people, who have the need to buy and the ability to pay for substantial amounts of your products and services than there are salespeople with the courage to ask them for an appointment.

Think about it; is a "no" from Mr. or Mrs. Big different than a "no" from Mr. or Mrs. Average, or, a "no" from Mr. or Mrs. Small?

A "no" from Mr. or Mrs. Big is significantly different because you've had the courage to call!

Mr. and Mrs. Big are the **Marlins** in the sea of prospects. Marlin are considered to be one of the best fighting fish in the world and greatly prized by sport fishermen. However, while there are millions of fishermen in the world, there are very few who have actually fished for and caught a marlin.

What's the point?

Well, the point is to separate yourself from the crowd, get out of your comfort zone, and be where the crowd isn't - fishing for **Marlin** and do so for just half an hour a week!

For just half an hour a week - remember the tiger!

My friends in Australia and New Zealand tell me that the best marlin fishing is when the weather is bad and the waves are rough.

Isn't that interesting .... for I believe that the best

time for us to approach Mr. or Mrs. Big to discuss their "financial plans for life", is when everyone else thinks that they will never give you an appointment because the salesperson's "mental winds" are too strong and the "waves in their mind" too high!

But, therein lies the opportunity! You see the time to call, the time to go **Marlin** fishing in business, is when everyone else says it can't be done. When the waves are too high and the winds are too strong!

Salespeople see Mr. or Mrs. Big in the paper and say "I'm going to call them, I'm going to call them." But, do they call them? In the vast majority of cases the answer is NO! (they never call them because they put off until "tomorrow" what is too uncomfortable for them to do today). And that's why the **Marlin** market is untapped!

How many of you run across competitors in the marketplace in which you are working? Lots? Try working the **Marlin** marketplace - there are very few sales people fishing it.

So, take a half an hour a week and go fishing for **Marlin**. Because while a "no" from Mr. or Mrs. Big is significantly different- so is a "yes". It may take you two, three, four, five years or more before you catch your first **Marlin**, but the glory, the honour, the nobility in trying is going to make you a much better "pan fisherman" in the process and the "dividends" from the **Marlin** itself won't be hard to take either!

> ***"Only those who attempt the absurd can achieve the impossible"***
> ***–Einstein***

> ***Prospect up!***
> ***Fish for Marlin***

Part II:

Separate Yourself From the Crowd

7. Outside The Square

Building a career in sales is like running a marathon.

Imagine a helicopter a thousand feet above the starting line taking pictures for the evening news.

After the race, you rush back to your hotel room to "see yourself on TV". Could you pick yourself out from the crowd? If the answer is "no", then, in the world of professional selling, how are your prospects supposed to pick you out from the crowd?

The crowd .... those hundreds of thousands of sales professionals who want to get in to see the prospect? How is the prospect going to separate you from the crowd? Ask yourself, how are you going to help the prospect separate you from the crowd?

You can separate yourself from your competitors by being different, by doing things differently, by thinking and conducting yourself differently, by doing the unexpected, by stepping outside of the square....

How are you at thinking outside of the square?

How do you join these nine dots with four straight connected lines?

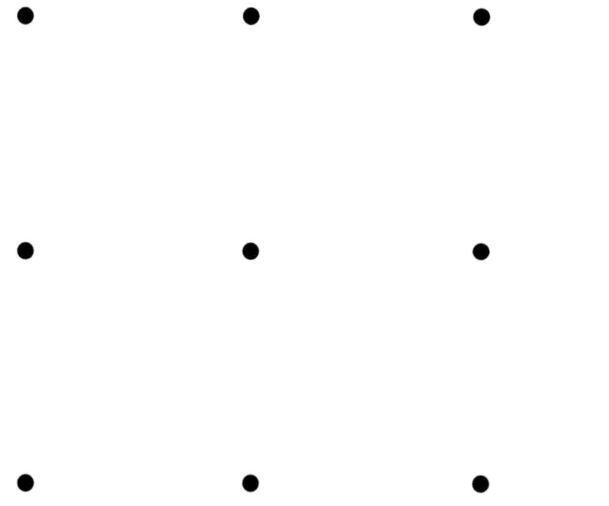

(Turn to the back of this book for the solution.)

8. Getting In

Here is a unique concept for "getting in." This concept is absolutely guaranteed to work...or not! (depending upon whether you choose to use it or not! .... where have you heard that before?)

When referred to John by Mark:

"Mark, would you be good enough to speak with John sometime in the next two, three weeks and tell him that he'll be receiving a letter from me?"

Mark always says yes, he'll be happy to do that. In reality, fifty percent of the time he does and 50% of the time he doesn't. However, in any event, send a pre-approach letter to John with a copy to Mark that says:

Wednesday, May 5

Dear John,

While we haven't met, Mark Adams, who is a friend and client of mine, speaks very highly of you.

As a result, I would like to meet you and thus plan to telephone you in the near future.

Yours sincerely,
Bruce Etherington

cc: Mark Adams

That's it! No enclosures, no coupons, no key-chains, no promises of free give-aways, or statements that we've helped everyone in the world including the last three national leaders!

The fact is, Mark has spoken very highly of John (by confirming that he does possess the three characteristics of a great referral) and we would like to meet him. Thus, our letter is straightforward and to the point, while at the same time, not giving Mark very much room to say "no".

When I was first in the business of selling life insurance, I was taught to send out a "pre-approach letter" and to follow it up immediately.

As a matter of fact, people around the world confirm, when asked, that very few sales people actually take the time to send pre-approach letters, and those that do, follow them up within a matter of a few days.

Rather than do that, try separating yourself from the crowd by not only sending a short and simple pre-approach letter, but also delay your follow-up for several weeks.

Why?

Well, do you really think, that this is what happens

when your letter is received by the prospect?...

"Mildred ... Look at this!" This is my lucky day, this is the most fantastic thing, a letter from a life insurance salesman. This is better than winning the lottery!!

When this highly skilled sales professional calls put him through! Give him the best spot on my calendar, I want to meet with him! I want to buy a million for me, half a million for my wife, a quarter of a million for each of my kids and probably a hundred thousand for my mother-in-law!!

This is a wonderful day!!"

Is that what happens? .... I don't think so!

In reality, isn't this how our prospects react when they receive our pre-approach letter?...

"Mildred, how long have you been with me? Twenty-four years. That's wonderful. I love you dearly Mildred, but do you see this letter? If this sales person gets in to see me, you are history!"

So...

The pre-approach letter prepares the prospect for your telephone call. Let's think about this.....if the prospect doesn't want to see you, then he or she is able to take the appropriate defensive measures to prevent you from getting in once they receive your letter. So why call when their guard is up?

Want proof? Well, how many of us have sent a pre-approach letter, followed it up immediately with a telephone call and been "zapped" by Mildred? You see Mildred is ready! As a matter of fact, she's ready on pain of her termination!!

What she has done is to surround herself with two U.S. army guard dogs, a bullet proof flak jacket, British army pith helmet, and her trusty AK-47! She is really ready and she is waiting for your call!

Are you prepared?

When the vast majority of people we are referred to don't initially want to meet with us, and go to creative lengths to prevent us from getting in, why would anyone walk into this trap?

So, we don't call right away and what happens over time is that Mildred's defences relax so much so, that after a few weeks our prospect's defences are down as well .... and .... that's when we call!

It's an incredible feeling of power when you pick up the phone and call an unsuspecting prospect, several weeks after sending the pre-approach letter and in the process .... totally ruin their day! (Just kidding!)

"Unsuspecting" only applies to the relaxation of his or her defence mechanisms, for Mildred has long ago returned the guard dogs to the pound and put away her flak jacket and machine gun.

John, our prospect, has either forgotten about you (thinking you are simply some disorganized sales person who forgot to call) or, in search of information, he has called Mark to ask him why in the world he has referred him to you!

Now, if the latter has happened that's good because it's an opportunity for third party influence to occur. But, if the former has taken place, which is more the likely, his preconditioning will allow you to move directly into your telephone approach when you call anywhere from four to six weeks later.

Marination

In your early days of selling, when you probably have but a few prospects and even fewer clients, you may feel that this technique may not be appropriate. However, once you use this tactic you will do so with great success if you just dare to be different and step out of your comfort zone!

You may also choose to graduate the strategy from a 2 to 3 week wait in the early days to a 6 to 8 week wait later on.

When you phone, four to six weeks later, your prospect has in all likelihood forgotten about you. As a matter of fact, when he/she first received your letter he probably wrote down all the reasons why he didn't want to see you: "I've bought enough.....my spouse can remarry......I'm not in the market.......I don't believe in life insurance"....whatever the myriad of excuses might be.

On the other hand, maybe, just maybe, Mark has called him and said a couple of nice things about you, or as mentioned he has called Mark and the same thing has happened......added spice to the marination!

Just as a beautiful piece of salmon tastes much nicer after it's had an opportunity to marinate, so will our prospect be much more receptive after he or she has marinated in the knowledge that they are going to receive a phone call from just about the last person in the world they want to hear from – you! (us!)

"The Call"

Here's the phone call .... (which again contains a phrase that is absolutely guaranteed to work .... or not!)

"Good morning, may I speak with Mark Adams please."

"Yes you may. May I ask who is calling?"

"Yes, it's Bruce Etherington."

"Is Mr. Adams expecting your call?"

"Well, yes as a matter of fact he's been expecting it for the last few weeks......"

"Adams here."

"Good morning Mark, it's Bruce Etherington calling, do you have a moment to talk on the phone?

"You're the guy .... you exist!"

"Mark, when in the next six to eight weeks do you think you and I can find a hour to meet one another.....?"

Now get ready to establish the **date**, the **time** and the **place.**

Let them marinate (the bigger the **Marlin!** the longer they marinate).

> ***Separate yourself from the crowd.***
>
> ***Marinate....***
>
> ***& ask:***
>
> ***"when in the next six to eight weeks can you and I find a hour to meet?...."***

Date. Time. Place.

In eighty percent of the cases, here is the response: "Six to eight weeks? Well, next week I'm out of town. The week after that is jammed, however, my calendar looks pretty good after that........".

#1. Fix the date

"Terrific. Would Monday the twentieth be good for you or would Wednesday the twenty-second suit you better?

"Well, Monday the twentieth looks relatively good."

#2. Fix the time

"Wonderful, Mark! Would 8:00 in the morning for breakfast be okay or would 12:00 noon for lunch suit you better?"

"12:00 noon looks good."

#3. Fix the place

"Fine Mark, now we are located at 170 University Avenue on the 7th floor and if you would be good enough to meet with me here, I would be delighted to host you for lunch."

"OK Bruce....."

"Great Mark, looking forward to seeing you on Monday the twentieth at 12:00 noon for lunch. Good-bye."

My assistant Edie will call Mark the day before the meeting to take his luncheon order (soup, salad, sandwich etc.) and give directions and location.

Thirty-eight years ago I was tired of evening appointments and asked my dad how to get day time meetings, to which he replied:

"Ask for them."

"Yes" I said, "but what else ?..... that's far to simple."

He replied:

"Ask for them".

And he was right!

Want your clients to come to your office? - Ask them.

Just as was said in the movie "Field of Dreams" - "if you build it, they will come"; so is the case with "in office" appointments - set up your office, invite your prospects to it and they will come.

Choices ….

Implied consent ….

Momentum!!!!

Offer choices to your clients, choices between two options, choices between "something and something" rather than "something and nothing".

We are not taking one huge quantum leap when we call for the appointment. We do not say: "Mark, I'm inviting you to come to my office on the twentieth of the month at 12:00 noon - see you then."

To which Mark could simply reply: "Forget it", as you have given him the choice between "something" and "nothing" and he has taken the "nothing".

Rather, we are taking this one step at a time (in the spirit of the tiger).....Date .... Time .... Place ... plus the choice between "something and something" rather than "something and nothing!"

In the vast majority of cases, the power of implied consent combined with the momentum of a series of positive choices (date, time and place) will fix the location of the meeting at your office.

Separate yourself from the crowd

#1. Date .... or ....

#2. Time .... or ....

#3. Place!

The "Yes" Highway

The purpose of asking questions is to build momentum in the form of dialogue with the prospect which is particularly important when attempting to acquire an appointment with this person whom you do not know but to whom you have been referred.

Thus, the opening—"Do you have a moment to talk on the phone?"—generally will result in a "Yes".

Let's build upon the "Yes".

"Did you receive my letter?" generally results in a response of "Yes".

Now these two, "Yesses" have in my mind mentally done two things. First of all, the first "Yes" positions my "sales car" on the "yes ramp" and the "yes ramp" leads me up into and onto the "yes lane" of the "yes highway" as opposed to the "no highway" which I want to avoid at all costs.

So, just to repeat for a moment –"Do you have a moment to talk on the phone?""Yes".

"Did you receive my letter?" "Yes".

"When in the next six to eight weeks do you think you and I can find a moment, an hour, to meet one another?" The first two "yesses" have put us in a position where now it is going to be very difficult for the prospect to reverse course, change lanes, and/or hop the median, onto the "no highway" because the "yes ramp" and the "yes lane" leads to the "yes highway". The prospect, by saying "yes" twice, has now committed himself to a "yes" pattern and thus, it has been my experience that eight out of ten prospects, to whom I have been referred, when asked these two questions in succession, following the receipt of a letter from me and introduction from a satisfied client, will agree to book an appointment with me and thus we are on the "yes highway" to sales success!

The Follow-up Note

Immediately following the telephone call, the appointment having been made, write a hand-written follow-up note that looks like this:

> *Dear John*
>
> *It was nice to chat with you today!*
>
> *Looking forward to meeting you Monday the twentieth, 12:00 noon here on the 7th floor for lunch. Edie will call to take your order.*
>
> *Yours sincerely,*
>
> *Bruce*

The hand-written note, again separates you from the crowd, in that it not only confirms your forthcoming luncheon date, but also represents a personal "outreach" to your new prospect, one that a computer generated letter can never duplicate.

(Note: if your hand writing like mine, is not very legible, then don't worry about it because your note in itself gives your prospect and/or client a reason to call you and ask "what did you say in your hand written letter"......?)

Another opportunity for contact!!

Separate yourself from the crowd! Use hand-written notes.

More "Requests for Reassurance"

20% to 30% of the time, when you follow-up your pre-approach letter, you will receive a "request for reassurance" following your opening statement, such as:
"Bruce, I appreciate your letter but I'm not in the market."

Or,

"Bruce, I appreciate your letter and strong reference from Mark, thank you very much but I'm well taken care of."

Or,

"Bruce, I'm really not interested."

Whatever the "request for reassurance", we have <u>one</u> answer: (which is also guaranteed to work or not)

"John, I can appreciate why you don't want to meet with me. However, let me be a little more specific about the reason why I sent you the letter and followed it up today with a phone call some two and a half months later.

By the way, I do apologize for the tardy follow-up, however, I know you're busy because we certainly are as well.......

Now John, the only reason I sent you the letter, was because Mark Adams, who is a good friend and client of mine, speaks very highly of you.

So much so, that he tells me that you possess three very unique characteristics that separate you from the crowd . Just before I hang up John, I thought you might like to know what those characteristics are.....

(Now, in 40 years of using this technique, I have never had anyone say: "don't bother! ")

So, interrupting the silence at the other end of the phone, you say:

"John, Mark tells me that you're a very responsible family and business person, who secondly, has the ability to make a decision that is based upon fact, not rumour; innuendo or hearsay and who, thirdly, has outstanding economic growth potential.

Now, quite frankly, if you didn't possess these three characteristics, I never would have sent you the letter nor followed it up with a phone call today. All I'd like to do John, is simply have the opportunity of meeting you, at some point down the road, in order to learn some specifics about you and your particular situation ..... strictly on a futures basis".

"So, ... John,..... would you have any objections to meeting me under those conditions?"

To which the vast majority of your prospects will reply:

"Well........ now that you put it that way........you know I'm not really in the market...........but if it's strictly on a "futures basis"......."

..... and the appointment is made!

You will book at least 80% of the people you call because you have taken the time to separate yourself from the crowd.

In the first year or two of my career I thought I didn't have the time to do all of this process as I was desperate for appointments and thus called a prospect as soon as I was referred or was able to "get the name." While I was able to get some appointments and make some sales, I now know that had I even used a variation of this methodology that I would have been able to get in to see a great deal more of my prospects and in fact probably have them come to my office sooner than was otherwise the case.

Over time as you grow in confidence and as your inventory of quality prospects grows larger, you will feel more confident in waiting longer to call and to casting further and further up stream. The key however is to begin to do something today with this strategy as over time, it will become more and more effective for you.

Separate Yourself....
Revised Revenue Example

- $1,000 per case
- See 8/10 and close 7/8
- Sales 70% x 60 prospects= 42

= $42,000 Revenue

Plus Future prospects....
This is the impact of 10-8-7 VS. 10-3-1.

Follow the process

One step at a time .....

#1. Letter and Marinate .....

#2. When within the next 6 - 8 weeks ... ?

#3. Date ..... Time ..... Place

#4. Momentum and Implied Consent

#5. Handwritten Note

9. The Avis List

What about the people we just can't get in to see? How do we separate ourselves from the crowd in that regard?

For years when I was in the "spear gun fishing" business and I couldn't get in to see a prospect after trying several different approaches, I would take their name and throw it away.

A big mistake!

To paraphrase Solomon:

> *"To everything there is a season.*
> *A time to plant and a time to harvest"*

And thus why not a time to lay fallow?

If this isn't the prospect's planting or growing time, then maybe, just maybe, we are calling at the wrong time.

How do we know that we are not approaching this person in their non-growing season, in their fallow season?

So, after we have said the words described in the previous chapter and John tells us a record twice:

"No thank you. I don't really want to meet with you"; this is the response:

"Well John, I can appreciate that. Obviously this is not a good time for us to be getting together and, as a result, what I'd like to do is this; I'd like to keep your name on file, with your permission, because things do have a way of changing and so, I'd like to stay in touch.

So John, would you have any objections, to allowing me to stay in touch with you over the years that lie ahead........?"

Seldom will John disagree with your suggestion and thus, he has automatically qualified for the ***Avis List***.

In North America, Avis, for years, has positioned itself as the "number two" car rental company. This led to the creation of an image of "trying harder" to win the customer's business.

Now, as far as John is concerned, I am somewhere down the list of professional advisors whom he wishes to meet and or have anything to do with.

Thus, just as Avis has to "try harder", so do I.

The ***Avis List*** is simply a special "bring forward" file that, each month, produces for me the names of people who one year ago said "no" to a request for a meeting with me.

So, up comes John's name on the ***Avis List*** one year later, at which time I pick up the phone and call John.

"Good morning, may I speak with John please?"

"Yes, may I tell him who's calling?"

"*Well, it's Bruce Etherington calling, however, I'd really appreciate it if you didn't tell John that I was calling because today is a special day in John's life and I have a very special surprise for him.........*"

"Smith here."

"Good morning John, it's Bruce Etherington calling, do you have a moment to talk on the phone?"

(Never ask "how are you", or anything like that as it is a potential invitation to disaster!

Why? Because what are you going to do on a positive basis if his response to "how are you" is "terrible".....?)

"Bruce who?"

"John, you recall a year ago, Mark Adams was kind enough to..."

"You're the insurance guy. I thought I told you a year ago, I'm not in the market! What are you calling me back for? Nothing's changed. I'm not interested."

"Well John, quite frankly, the reason I'm calling you today is to wish you 'Happy Anniversary'"!

"What are you talking about?"

"Well John, it was exactly one year ago today that I first called and you told me you didn't want to meet with me .... and so .... I'm simply calling you today to wish you 'Happy Anniversary' on this the first year of our non-relationship!"

"You've got to be kidding.....!!"

"John, to everything there is a season .... and so ... I'm calling to ask you, when in the next six to eight weeks do you think that we can find an hour to meet one another..........?"

In nine out of ten situations the ice is broken, the prospect loosens up, enjoys a laugh and realizes in the process that he or she is dealing with someone who definitely is operating "outside of the square!"

Separate yourself from the crowd!

Make your Avis List

Be persistent

&

Have fun!!!

10. Chris' Story

Chris was on my ***Avis List*** for six and a half years! Just before the sixth year anniversary, at Christmas time, I received the following fax:

Tuesday, December 5

Dear Bruce,

Merry Christmas!

Don't bother!

Sincerely,
Chris

How wonderful - we'd become fax pals! For six years he had said "no" and now we had a fax relationship going. However, because he had trumped me with his pre-empting fax, I needed to change tactics:

So, at the six and a half year anniversary, I called and he said:

"You're early!"

"Yes Chris, I'm six months early.......I had to change tactics because you scooped me at Christmas."

"OK, time out, I'll come in."

"You will?"

"Yes, I've put you through enough, I've deferred you long enough. I'm coming in."

He came across the street two weeks later. He was, and still is, a successful entrepreneur. He said:

"Time out, time out!"

"What is it, Chris?"

"I know what you are going to do in this first meeting. You are going sit me down and ask me a lot of questions. Then, in the second meeting, you're going to use your easel, some slides, charts and pictures and probably try to sell me something. And that's fine, however, I want to just "cut to the quick": I'm telling you right now that if you can come up with one reason, during our meetings, why we should do business together then I'll buy from you."

"You will......?"

"Absolutely!"

"Well, why would you tell me that after it took me six and a half years to get you in here?"

"Bruce, that's precisely the point. If you service me with half of the intensity and passion with which you have pursued me, then I will be one of the best looked after people in town."

Chris became a valued client. However, without the ***Avis List*** we never would have done any business......think about it......"To everything there is a season....", how many excellent prospects do you have whom you've initially contacted in the wrong season.....?

Years later at 51, following a regular early morning tennis match, Chris suffered a heart attack.

Three months later, we were having lunch in his office and he said:

"Bruce, there's something I want you to share with every insurance group to which you speak. I want you to know what happened after my heart attack.

The company that I was negotiating a merger with called my office and subsequently offered to buy my business for 15 cents on the dollar!

My wife didn't want to tell me that because she thought that it would have a negative effect on my health, so, she lived with that knowledge for thirty days until I got out of intensive care, and then she told me.

I was so upset .... and then I calmed down when I realized that I didn't have to sell. You see, ... as you've told me for years, when I die, my family is not going to get fifteen cents on the dollar for the business, they are going to get 100 cents on the dollar because of my life insurance program.

Furthermore, if I remain disabled, I will receive 75 cents on the dollar for the business and an income for life as well!

Finally, if I don't get any better I've got time to sell the business for at least 50 to 70 cents on the dollar, which combined with my disability income and pension plan gives me financial peace of mind.

So Bruce, while we haven't filled out any claim forms here today, I want you to know the impact that your concepts, products and services have had on me and my family.

They have prevented a 'fire sale', and kept my business together, for which I am very grateful."

So, what's the point?

Well ..... years ago I would have thrown Chris's name away after the first telephone call when he initially refused to meet with me.

But when you cast upstream, when you are patient, when you give your sense of humour a chance to work, when you dare to step out of your comfort zone and separate yourself from the crowd..... that's when the magic happens!

Remember:

"Think

Believe

Dream

Dare"

&

Create magic

with your Avis List

11. Top Down Selling

Work with the decision maker.

If you do not speak with a decision maker, you will not get a decision.

Over several years I shifted my business from the individual to the corporate market with my brother. We targeted corporations for employee benefit and pension plans.

Everyone in the pensions and benefits consulting field told us:

"You must deal strictly with the Vice President of Human Relations, or the Vice President of Benefits. You'll never be able to talk to the CEO of the company about a benefits or disability package, or about their pension plan. They're just not interested."

So, we listened to them. For the first six months we had all kinds of wonderful meetings with many VP's of this and many VP's of that, and we had absolutely no positive results! So, we altered our strategy, and started to do what we had done for many years in the personal marketplace.......**we invited the decision maker, the COO, President or CEO, to come to our office for the first meeting.**

When we approached the corporate decision makers, the ***Requests for Reassurance*** that we received were as follows:

"Bruce, I know Mark speaks highly of you and I know that you've been able to help his company but I don't look after this. I have a VP that looks after pensions and benefits, so, I would be happy to have you call her"....

"John, while I appreciate the fact that it's your VP Finance who reviews your employee benefit or pension plans, our mutual friend Mark Johnson referred me to you and not to your VP. So, before

we get too specific about benefit or pension plans, I would simply like to meet you.

When in the next six to eight weeks, can you and I find an hour to meet one another?"

"Well, Bruce, what would the meeting be about?"

"John, the purpose of our meeting is to allow me to learn something about you and vice versa. So, how's your calendar over the next six to eight weeks?.....".

"Well Bruce, I don't really think that this would be a particularly good use of my time."

"Well, John, I can appreciate that, however just as you don't look after the details of your benefit package which you leave to your staff, so do I with mine. All I'd like to do is learn something about you and your particular situation .... so, would you have any objections to meeting with me under that condition?"

"Well, now that you put it that way....."

"Fine John, when in the next six to eight weeks can we find an hour to meet?"

Take a stand and not an order!

When you are referred to the President, the CEO, the decision maker - that's who you want to meet!

Just as in the personal marketplace when you are referred to a particular person if that individual said: "Well, I want you to talk to my accountant first .... or I want you to talk to my lawyer first ...."

Wouldn't we try to meet with the person to whom we have been referred? I know I would, because we both have the same objective and that is to build relationships with people as a result of which will eventually come, in all likelihood, business.

However, if we don't get to see the people to whom we have been referred, it's highly unlikely that we'll ever get to make a sale!

So, get the CEO's and the Presidents in your office. Why? Because very few people are doing that. Step outside of the square, ask and you will receive. Don't ask and you won't get! (By the way, quite often they will bring their VP's with them and that is fine! The key is to get them in!)

Believe me "top down selling" works

We tracked it over twelve years and found that we sold seven out of ten corporations a product or a service within twelve months of the first meeting, at which the President and/or CEO, generally accompanied by their VP's, came to our office for the first meeting.

So figure it out. If you can get eighty percent of your referrals in your office and you sell ninety percent of them in the first year, that's 72% of your referrals resulting in business within twelve months of obtaining the introduction!

Separate yourself from the crowd.

Top down marketing.

Deal with the decision maker.

Take a stand and

not an order!

12. The Deal Before the Deal

This is absolutely guaranteed to eliminate all competition! (As long as you're dealing with quality people.)

The Deal Before the Deal is absolutely guaranteed to elevate the impression that your prospect has of you, regardless of how strong your reference has been, right from the opening moments of your first meeting.

"John, I want to thank you for meeting with me today. In the next hour or so we're going to 'break a little bread' and chat. What I'd like to do is ask a lot of questions about you and your business, based upon three conditions:

The first condition is that any information you share with me will be kept by me in the strictest of confidence.

The second condition is that we'd like to have some time, John, to think about the information that you share with us; because if we don't feel that we can be of any help to you I will tell you so and save your time as well as ours.

The third condition, is that if we do meet again and share ideas and concepts with you that you like, and which you ultimately decide to implement, then we would expect you to do so with our firm and not with anyone else in our business.

Are you comfortable with this, John?"

99% of your prospects will say "Fair enough" and you have their verbal agreement, or "handshake" on ***The Deal Before the Deal***.

For the 1% who says :

"Well, no. I'm not comfortable with that, I'd really like to go out and get some quotes. I've got to shop the market."

We say:

"I can appreciate that but why?"

If their "why" doesn't make any sense or is based strictly upon "shopping, shopping, shopping" for the sake of shopping, then....

"Let's finish our sandwich and chat for a minute anyway. You should definitely go and shop the market, and after you have shopped and researched and you know exactly what you are looking for, in terms of product, price and structure then come back and see us and we'll try this again."

You see this process is designed to filter out people who may simply want to take your ideas and run. Thus, **The Deal Before the Deal** puts your operating parameters squarely on the table and leaves no room for the prospect to wonder what is going to happen and what your expectations are as a result.

The choice is yours. Try it and see how it works for you. Don't try it and continue to expose yourself to what each of us has experienced after finding a prospect, researching the case, making a presentation only to hear at the end:

"Bruce, I really like this idea, but I promised my old university roommate, or I promised my cousin, Harry, that I would talk over any insurance or financial planning recommendation with them before I bought anything. You see, I really have to give them a chance to quote on the business, and while I really like everything you have done for me I'm sure that you can appreciate that if you were in my position you would probably have to do the same thing."

I don't know about you, but that situation occurred on many occasions particularly when I was a young salesman and it nearly drove me crazy until during a conversation with my dad, who himself was an outstanding sales professional, the seeds of the "deal before the deal" were sown.

So try it, it works, it'll simplify your life, enhance your enjoyment and magnify your sales!

Separate yourself from the crowd.

Use the Deal Before the Deal.

13. The Three Year Question

The most powerful question I have ever asked any prospective client in a fact finding meeting is a version of Dan Sullivan's (The Strategic Coach), "Relationship Question" which I call, with Dan's permission, "The Three Year Question."

"John, if we were sitting here three years from today on (insert date), looking back over the previous three years to today, what would have to have happened in your business (professional) and personal lives over that period of time, in order for you to feel that you had made good to excellent progress?"

The longest answer I have had to this question was 59 minutes, the shortest was 30 seconds.

The gentleman who answered in just under an hour became a client, while the lady who gave me the 30 second answer, did not.

In both cases however the answers revealed to me exactly what their priorities in life were at that point in time. the priorities of the gentleman caused us to be able to add value to his situation and thus he became a client, while the priorities of the lady did not present us an opportunity to so do.

The beauty of this question is that it focuses on what's important to the prospect and, in order for us to properly serve the prospect, this, as you know, we need to know.

The reaction to this question has been so positive over the past 15 years since I began using it that I have, in many cases, simply allowed the fact finding interview, which normally runs 1 1/2 to 2 1/2 hours, to flow from this question, because what it will do is take you to the heart of the clients interest, concerns, likes, dislikes, fears, wants, goals and objectives and allow your entire discussion to flow from there.

It also gets you totally away from the standard routine, "hard/fact, dry information" type of fact finding that financial institutions have virtually to a corporation trained their advisors to use.

This allows the advisor to enjoy the flow of information, passion, interests and concerns from the client while allowing the prospective client to relax and focus on their concerns and objectives, thus creating an atmosphere of individuality and specific personal concern, as opposed to the rote and formulaic approach of a numerically based fact finding meeting.

I would encourage you to memorize the "Three Year Question" and by so doing realize the benefits of discipline which are very clearly summarized in a scripture from the book of Hebrews "No discipline seems pleasant at the time but painful. Later on however it produces a harvest of righteousness and peace for those who have been trained by it."

In essence, the discipline which we apply to our selling skills is not any different from that which a professional athlete applies to their sport. We want to "groove our swing" so that regardless of the wind and weather conditions it will be virtually the same on as many occasions as it can be and while we know that it is practiced and rehearsed, it comes across very clearly as an original statement to the prospect.

In the pressure of the first interview, wherein which the sales advisor is certainly operating in new territory, as far as his or her relationship is concerned with the prospect, the least said by the sales advisor generally generates the best results. As God has given us one mouth and two ears it is time in this first interview to use the two ears twice as much as we use the one mouth. By opening with the "Three Year question" this allows our prospective client to truly share with us what is important to them and when we know what is important to them we have an opportunity to subsequently "add value".

14. How to Deal With Voice And E-Mail

Attempting to make contact with a prospect today is, in my opinion, much more difficult than it was 40 years ago, pre voice and e-mail.

Yes, then we had gatekeepers of the day who were very effective at "protecting" their bosses from the advances of aggressive sales people. However, I did find in the '70s, '80s and '90s, up until the arrival of voicemail, that the strategies which I have shared with you to this point in time worked extremely well, in fact they still do. However, we must be prepared to deal with two additional weapons which the gatekeeper has at her disposal and which her boss, our prospect, can utilize very effectively. Let's address them.

Voicemail

Rather than looking at voicemail as a weapon that can be used exclusively on a defensive basis by the gatekeeper, let's consider it to be an additional arrow in our quiver of tools with which we may gain access to and ultimately meet the prospect to whom we have been referred.

When I telephone a prospect, having followed to the letter the procedures outlined in this book and encounter voicemail, this is what I do:

I leave a message. Voicemail, I believe, is looked upon by the senior executive and/or business owner today, as an effective, time saving vehicle for the exchange and gathering of information. Thus, I intend to leave him or her some information:

- the fact that I did follow up the letter
- the fact that I called today
- the fact that I am interested in meeting with them

- the fact that I do come highly referred from the person who referred me to them and vice versa
- the fact that I am busy
- the fact that I do not have all the time in the world to see them but can allocate some, i.e. a portion, of my busy time to their calendar, subject to our mutual agreement
- the fact that I am pleasant, sound bright and interesting on the telephone and have a professional follow up with out any overly aggressive sales "pitch".

How does this translate to the voicemail message? Well, let's suppose I have sent a letter to a business owner and upon following it up a month or two later, as per the methodology outlined in this book, I encounter voicemail. This is the type of message I will leave:

"Mary, it's Bruce Etherington calling. As you may recall, Don Robinson has introduced us. A few weeks ago I took the liberty of sending you a let-

ter which I am following up today. There isn't any urgency to us meeting however, I would like to have, at some point in time, the opportunity of meeting you as Don speaks very highly of you. Thus, I will leave my number and if you have the opportunity to do so please return my call and we can work towards setting a mutually convenient date to meet one another. Looking forward to hearing from you soon..., Bruce Etherington and the number is 416-351-1464. Thanks.

Now, generally, in many cases that does not garner a response. However, once again, depending upon the strength of the referral, in several cases it does and I have been pleasantly surprised to receive a phone call back in a day or two from the prospect saying, yes, they did get the call. Yes, they have talked with Don and yes, they would be pleased to meet. However that will happen about maybe 30% of the time. In the other 70% of these situations I follow up and this prospect's name now goes on "two week follow up" and for the first three calls I will call this prospect once every two weeks. After that, I will call them once a week. Here is a sample:

"Hi, Mary. It's Bruce Etherington calling. You may recall receiving a phone message from me about two weeks ago as a result of an introduction from Don Robinson. If you would be good enough to call me back at 416-351-1464, Extension 22, I would love to set a date to meet with you."

Let's suppose we still haven't heard from Mary two weeks later. Here is the next call:

"Hi, Mary. Bruce Etherington calling again. Don't mean to bother you but I certainly would like to meet you, particularly in view of all of the good things that Don Robinson has had to say about you. Hopefully we will be able to meet at some future point but in the meantime, if you would be good enough to return my call we can set a date. Actually, I would be also happy to hear from your assistant. She could also call my Assistant, Edie Helliwell, our Director of Client Relations at 416-351-1464 Ext 21."

Now, what we have here is dialogue. We are communicating with their voicemail but nobody has called me back from her office at this point to tell me to stop, cease, desist and not do this again, which simply means to me that this prospect is now running me through his or her "filter".

Every affluent prospect, in fact every prospect, runs a sales person through their filter. The "persistence filter". How persistent is this individual going to be? In other words, why should I invest my valuable time with this particular sales person? If I don't have an answer to that then, quite frankly, I don't think I will bother calling back. Let's see how many times they call me before I call them, every individual has their own grade of filters, it's like buying coffee filters at the supermarket, some people have a #1 grade filter, one return phone call, and they will call you back. Others have a #4 grade, they want you to call them four times and then they will call you back. Others have a #8 grade etc.

As I have shared with you in the story of Chris and the Avis list, his "coffee filter" was several years long!

An interesting side bar story is Tom, with whom I had an ongoing voicemail dialogue for over four years, and one day I picked up the newspaper and saw that Tom, a very successful and extremely wealthy businessman, had had a heart attack while on vacation and died at the age of 58. Now whether or not Tom actually needed my services, I don't know, but what that fact reinforced in my mind was that good health is a day to day possession and that sooner or later all of us are going to "graduate to the next dimension" and leave this one!

I do not know, and will not know, if I can add value as a practitioner until I sit down in front of the prospect. The financial planning world is full of examples of the rich and famous, many of whom died leaving pennies in their estates and, in many cases, having their families incur utter financial ruin and embarrassment. While they were in the public eye, nevertheless, the privacy of their finances had been so well guarded that no one had ever been able to properly structure them and as a result, much was lost through bad business decisions, investments and or the impact of taxation.

So, do not be fooled by the public persona of an individual. If they possess the three significant characteristics that we seek in a prospect, namely - responsibility, the ability to make decisions, and good to excellent economic resources - then they are prospects and candidates for you, particularly if they come highly recommended by one of your valued clients.

On the other hand, the number of situations where I have ultimately gained appointments with people through identifying and communicating with them via voicemail is extraordinary. So, use voicemail as an ally. Use it as an additional tool in your marketing quiver because it can be an extremely effective arrow with which to let your message fly to the heart of the targeted prospect.

E-mail

E-mail is an interesting phenomena. It is both a blessing and a curse, as we all know. So, let's talk about how it can be a blessing in gaining access to quality, affluent people.

Quite often, when I send my introductory letter, I will send two versions of that letter. Namely, a "snail mail" traditional, signed, stationary embossed letter and an e-mail version as well. Thus, when I follow up with the prospect, as we have just discussed with the medium of voicemail, I am able to use both hand written, traditionally typed and/or e-mail correspondence with that individual to continue to build a relationship prior to meeting them.

I think of this as drawing strings and then ropes and then cables across a chasm in the construction of a bridge. The first piece of material that crosses the canyon or chasm or gulch or river is in essence a string or a small rope which pulls behind it a larger rope which ultimately pulls a cable and then the construction of the bridge follows.

Our prospect letter, regardless of the form which it takes, is the string. The telephone call is the rope. The voicemail message is another rope. Subsequent follow-ups via e-mail and/or voicemail contacts are additional strands which are crossing the chasm until ultimately the personal contact and the telephone appointment call/discussion is the cable which, in eight out of ten cases, results in an appointment being acquired and the bridge being built.

Let's remember that the sole objective of the telephone call is to get an appointment, nothing other than to <u>get the appointment</u>.

Thus, my e-mail communications will follow, mirror and accentuate my voicemail messages and I may, every two weeks, send a voicemail and then two weeks later send an e-mail. Let's look at an example:

Let's suppose we are now one month into the post initial telephone call phase and I have left two voicemails for this prospect. This time, it being the sixth week after my initial call, I will leave an e-mail which might look like this:

Dear Mary:

Further to my last couple of voicemails, I thought I would try to reach you via the magic of e-mail. As you may recall, Don Robinson has suggested that we meet. While I have been very privileged to act for Don I have also learned to take the advice and guidance of my valued clients seriously and that is the reason why I continue to attempt to reach you. Since Don speaks so highly of you, I would like to meet you and thus would appreciate hearing back from you at some point, wherein which we will be able to arrange to meet sometime over the next six to eight to ten to twelve weeks.

Looking forward to that opportunity and to talking with you soon.

Yours sincerely,

Two weeks after that I may send a hand written note that says the same thing but the key is, that we can build rapport, send information, add credibility about ourselves, i.e. our CV, reference and access to our website, nice personal note about mutually shared interests etc. via e-mail. It is a recognized fact that the demographic statistics have shown that people who communicate with each other via e-mail generally have stronger relationships with each other than otherwise would be the case...even if they do not see each other that often!

Thus I have found that e-mail communication with prospects, post my initial letter and telephone call can be and is extremely effective.

Hand Written or Typed?

The pre approach letter can be either hand written or typed - you choose.

In many, many cases, and for most of my career I have sent typed pre approach letters and attached my CV (bio).

In some cases, today I send the letter and enclose our brochure.

In other cases, I simply send the letter, either typed or hand written.

There is nothing wrong with a hand written introductory letter, however, for hand written notes I would rather send a hand written greeting or note card with my company logo etc. on it than a hand written piece of stationary but, on the other hand, a hand written piece of stationary is fine. You judge the nature of the client and you might even ask your client who refers you to this prospect, what do you think they would appreciate and like the most, a typed or hand written note? Of course, if you are e-mailing the letter it is tough to send an e-mail copy of a hand written note, on the other hand, you could send the hand written note with a PS on it that says "PS An e-mail copy of this will also be coming to you", i.e. creativity and flexibility.

Be creative and enjoy the process!

15. Just The Facts ... Listen And Learn

Dr.Thomas Stanley in his excellent book "Marketing to the Affluent" makes the following two key points:

#1. The super sales professional asks a lot of questions and listens to the answers.

#2. The super sales professional, asks for the order, ...again .... and .... again .... and .... again .... and again."

Maybe not in the same meeting, maybe not in the same month, maybe not in the same quarter, or in the same year, but they ask "again and again and again and again and again"... until in the vast majority of cases, they get the order.

Let's examine Dr. Stanley's points.

What's so important about asking questions and listening to the answers?

Well, let's suppose you went to see your doctor for your annual physical. Before you have even had a chance to say hello, in sweeps the doctor saying: "Hi Mark, how are you? Take off your jacket".

Suddenly he comes at you with a foot long gleaming hypodermic - dripping at the end. He says "roll up your sleeve" and before you've said a word he's swabbing your arm. Finally you blurt out:

"Hey doc, what are you doing?"

"What do you mean what am I doing? If I do 50 of these a week for the next six weeks I win a free trip to Hawaii!"

Do you think you might change doctors?!

What's the point .... ?

How many of us are out there in the marketplace with loaded "hypodermics" or "spear guns", sharpened and ready to go, with an attitude of: "Don't confuse me with the facts, I'm just here to make the sale!"

Want relationships? Get the facts at the beginning. "Ask and you shall receive."

You see, when a prospect meets you for the first time they really expect that you are going to try to sell them something. When you invest two hours getting the facts, listening to them talk about their favourite subject - themselves, the prospect will leave the meeting thinking: "I've just met a sales person that didn't ask me to buy something. I spent two hours with them sharing more about me than anyone knows .... and they didn't even ask me to buy anything, this is unbelievable!"

Do you think they're going to come back to see what you do with that information. You bet they will!

> *"A wise person considers the facts, and plans accordingly, while a simpleton ignores them and pays the consequences."*
>
> *Proverbs*

Separate yourself from the crowd!

Throw your spear gun and hypodermic away.

Get the facts!

Listen & learn!

16. Activity

Activity- another way to separate yourself from the crowd.

The reason most people don't reach the pinnacle of sales achievement in whatever business they are in, is because they either don't have enough quality people to see, or if they do, they are not seeing enough of them!

How many people a week do you see?

What is your average revenue per sale?

What is your annual sales objective?

Does the average revenue per sale multiplied by the number of sales you make equal your sales objective? If it doesn't, then you need to either increase the number of quality people you see, or increase the size of each sale you make, or both!

Let's suppose your objective is to see three people a day.

Up until the time I was 33, I attempted to see six people a day and between twenty five to thirty people a week. Then from 33-43 I shifted to four people a day, and at 53 to 3 people a day. Now at 63 I can't do what I once did at 33. As a matter of fact, anyone who tells you they can do at 63 what they once did at 33, didn't do a lot at 33!

So now in my business, we aim for eight appointments a week, two a day for four days from Tuesday through Friday, leaving Monday for administration, case prep, staff meetings and all of the details that are required to run a business.

At nine o'clock we have muffins and juice, coffee or tea, at twelve o'clock sandwiches or salad and at four o'clock cookies and tea.

Schedule: Tuesday to Friday		
	AM	**Appointment**
9:00	AM	
10:00	AM	
11:00	AM	
12:00	PM	**Appointment**
1:00	PM	
2:00	PM	
3:00	PM	
4:00	PM	**Appointment**
5:00	PM	

Why do we always have food? Have you noticed what happens to the conversation level when food is shared? It seems physiologically impossible but the voice level goes up when the mouth is full!

When you think about it, how can the prospect get upset with you when his or her mouth is full of **your tax free muffin!**

So, 2 sales related meetings a day times four days equals eight selling situations a week. They could be openings, fact findings, conceptual presentations, closings, deliveries, public relations and/or service related sessions, all of which are designed to promote, develop and enhance our overall professional relationship.

Here's an example of how this daily scheduling may impact your business in the early years, when you are still growing and learning your selling skills:

Total booked appointments (3/day):	12
Cancellations per week: (33%)	4
Number of weekly meetings:	8
Closing ratio:	1 in 3
Number of weekly sales:	2.7
Number of productive weeks per year:	40
Number of annual sales:	**108**

Have you made 100 or more sales in the past year?

Has anyone failed in the life insurance, money market, financial planning, employee benefit, pension and/or securities business because they only made 100 sales in one year?

I don't think so!

As the quality and calibre of the people you meet improves, fewer will cancel. Similarly, your closing ratio will improve over time because of your experience and expertise combined with the quality and financial resources of your prospects. Thus, here's how your business might look a few years later:

Total booked appointments:	12
Cancellations per week: (25%)	3
Number of weekly meetings:	9
Closing ratio:	1 in 2*
Number of weekly sales:	4.5
Number of productive weeks per year:	40
Number of annual sales:	**180**

**Dr. Stanley's second point-"ask".*

That's Mount Everest country!

In my 20's, 30's and early 40's I averaged well over 150 sales a year, year after year after year after year. Build your base!

Now in my sixties I'm averaging 50 sales annually in a 25 week year.

Total booked appointments:	8
Cancellations per week: (25%)	2
Number of weekly meetings:	6
Closing ratio:*	1 in 3
Number of weekly sales:	2
Number of productive weeks per year:	25
Number of annual sales:	**50**

* *Average case now requires six meetings*

However, we must remember that you can't do with "oak trees", what you once did with "acorns" or little "saplings," since our established clients will require more time as their situations and circumstances become more complex. Thus, you've got to be able to find the time to cultivate them, as well as to work with them in order to help them help themselves.

Pruning

We have previously talked about pruning your garden. But, in order to have something to prune you first of all must plant. Be it a garden or a forest, be careful of what you plant, because as the Bible says:

"You will reap what you sow."

Some day we are all probably going to want to have some relief from the sun; the heat of the action, the toil of the vineyard. When we do, what kind of shade will we have?

Look at the trees you are planting today and ask yourself will they provide the "economic shade" that you may well want in your fifties, sixties seventies, eighties and beyond?

The choice is yours!

Get active and see the people, for "ideas are a dime a dozen but the person who puts them into practice can create millions!"

3 people a day

X

4 days =

12 meetings ("opportunities")

per week!

17. SWEAT!

For me, five letters say it all:

Sights!

In the words of Robert Frost:

> *"I shall be telling this with a sigh,*
> *somewhere ages and ages hence.*
> *Two roads diverged in a wood and I,*
> *I took the one less travelled by,*
> *and that has made all the difference."*

All the difference .... we really can make all the difference.

To paraphrase Ernie Banks' opening remarks at the 1992 Million Dollar Round Table meeting in Chicago:

"Life is like a baseball diamond. First base represents our physical conditioning, second base our mental state, third base our social life and home plate our spiritual life."

As for me, my sights were "blurred" until my friend Sam Williams introduced me to Canadian hockey hero Paul Henderson, now a lay minister in Toronto with Campus Crusade for Christ. Paul challenged me in January 1987 when he asked: "Bruce, how is your spiritual life?"

At that time business was "number one", my wife, Karen, and children, Michael, Sarah and Jay, were "number two" and my friends and God followed in that order.

In addition, while I had enjoyed tremendous success in the profession of selling, I was "under the pile" with a major business headache abroad.

As a result of Paul's question, my circumstances at the time, and the subsequent re-focusing of my sights over the past few years, my priorities as a Christian are now:

God, and His Son Jesus Christ my Lord and Saviour, family, health, friends and business.

And, funny thing .... business has never been better!

As the prophet Jeremiah said:

"God has a plan for you, a plan for good and not for evil, a plan with a future and a hope."

As the late great John Savage said "If you don't have a spiritual life, get one!"

Sights. Where are yours?

Work.

> *"For to seek grand results without great effort, you are a fool even to desire it."*
>
> ***Thomas Jefferson***

Look at the great athletes.

When Steve Podborski was asked how a kid who learned to ski on a six hundred foot vertical hill in southern Ontario, could go on to become the World Cup downhill racing champion, he replied: "..... I worked at it."

When Paul Henderson, the hero of the 1972 Canada - Russia hockey summit, was asked how he made it to the NHL, he said: " ....I really worked at my skating. I practiced, practiced and practiced....".

Pick a sport, look at its champions:

Basketball: Brian Heaney, Michael Jordan, Steve Nash

Baseball: Joe DiMaggio, Hank Aaron, Paul Molitor

Cricket: Sir Gary Sobers, Brian Lara

Football: Joe Montana, Doug Flutie, Damon Allen

Golf: Jack Nicklaus, Ben Hogan, Tiger Woods

Hockey: Wayne Gretzky, Mario Lemieux, Steve Yzerman

Rugby: David Campese

Sailing: John Bertram, Dennis Connor

Squash: Heather McKay

Skiing: Jean-Claude Killy, Franz Klammer, Kate Pace Lindsay

Soccer: Pele, Sir Stanley Matthews

Tennis: Chris Evert, Andre Agassi, Pete Sampras

Track and Field: Sir Roger Bannister, Carl Lewis, Donovan Bailey

Whether it's sport, family, community or business, the truth in life is:

"The only time success comes before work is in the dictionary."

Enthusiasm.

From the Greek, "en theos" - "God within".

> *"Success is never final and failure is never fatal. The key to victory is to soldier on with enthusiasm."*
> *- Sir Winston Churchill*

My dad often said:

"In order for the prospect to be lukewarm, the salesperson has to be red hot."
Can you think of one person whom you know who is outstanding in their field and not enthusiastic about what it is they do? .... think about it.

Be enthusiastic!

Sir Winston also said that he never felt more enthusiastic about life as when he was shot at and missed!

Attitude. Is your glass half full or half empty?

> *"It's your attitude and not your aptitude that will determine your altitude."*

We've been told that over and over and over again but, isn't it the truth?

As Napoleon Hill wrote in his wonderful book, "Think and Grow Rich" ....

> *"whatever the mind of man can conceive and believe he can achieve"*

.... how else do you explain Neil Armstrong's walk on the moon?

Tenacity.

In his later years, Sir Winston Churchill was invited to give the graduation address at Harrow, his boyhood school. After a lengthy introduction, this greatest of Englishmen, turned and faced the assembled school boys: pausing, he said:

"Never ... never .... never ..... never ...... never .... NEVER .... give up!"

Whereupon he sat down and received a standing ovation.

Think about it ...

Isn't it true that every great accomplishment was once considered an impossibility?

Or, How about:

St. Paul .... Michelangelo .... Christopher Columbus .... Joan of Ark, ...Mother Theresa .... Martin Luther King ... Terry Fox .... Bob Wieland .... Nelson Mandela .... Anne Frank .... Abraham Lincoln .... Captain Cook .... Ben Feldman ...

.... great people .... who accomplished great things .... in the face of great adversity.

> *"I can promise you nothing but*
> *blood, toil, tears and sweat!"*
> *- Churchill*

> *"No one has ever drowned in a pool of*
> *their own sweat".*
> *- Ron Barbaro*

Tenacity is belief and desire,
with passion on fire!

Never ... ever... give up!

So;

Focus your . . . . **S**IGHTS
Go to . . . . **W**ORK
Be . . . . **E**NTHUSIASTIC
Have a positive . . . . . **A**TTITUDE
Be . . . . **T**ENACIOUS

You ***"SWEAT"***, I'll ***"SWEAT"*** and together, we'll "***SEE THE PEOPLE***" and enjoy the results!

About The Author

Born in England and educated in Canada, Bruce Etherington has entertained and inspired sales people around the world. His humorous and direct style enhances his unique transferable sales strategies that help people significantly expand their businesses.

Bruce's ***"Client Building System"*** has evolved over his 41 years in the life insurance business. In addition to his financial planning practice in Toronto where he utilizes all of the strategies and techniques he describes in this book, Bruce also dedicates a substantial amount of time to teaching and motivating sales people with his "outside the square" relationship based sales concepts.

Now in his 38th year as a "Life and Qualifying" member of the financial advisorial industry's most prestigious organization, The Million Dollar Round Table; Bruce is also a Charter and 29 year Qualifying member of the Top of the Table, (which is comprised of the top 1/5 of 1% of life insurance sales people in the world), of which he was the 1993 Chairman.

Bruce's mission is to "help others help themselves". As a result, he is dedicated to helping sales people enhance their skills and become more effective as they ***"See the People"***.

Active in his community, he is father to Michael, Jay and Sarah, and father-in-law to Dave and grandfather to Lucas. Bruce resides in Oakville, Ontario with his best friend and wife of 38 years, Karen.

Solution to the nine dot square puzzle:

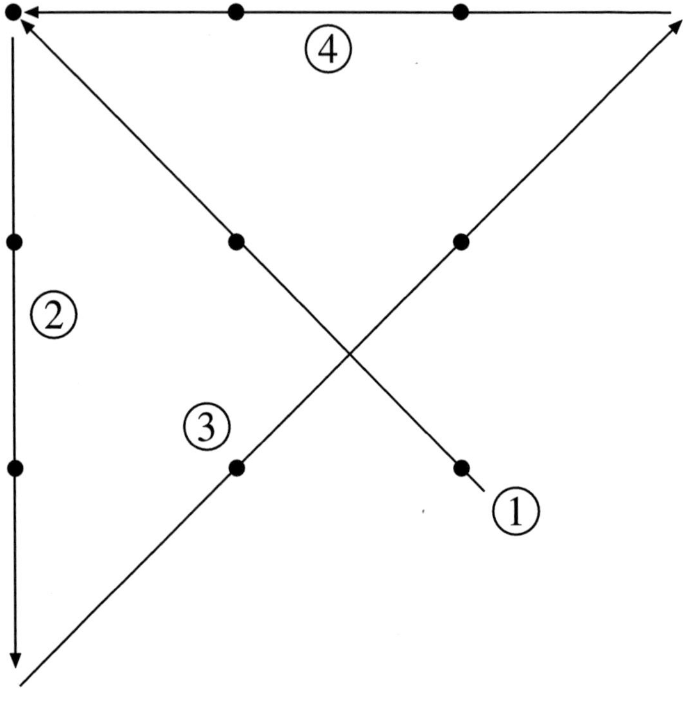